AMERICA
Rosary

TO UNITE THE
I AM RACE
IN THE LINEAGE OF THE ANCIENT OF DAYS

This publication is a Call to Action for the
I AM Race—the sons and daughters of God of every race
and nation, all children of the Light, those of the lost Twelve Tribes,
and the 144,000 to invoke the divine intercession required to
achieve their full and final Declaration of Independence from
spiritual and political tyranny and for the victory of planet earth.

Released for the July 4ᵗʰ celebrations in the year 2012, the 236ᵗʰ
Anniversary of the signing of the Declaration of Independence
of the United States of America

Written and Compiled by

Alberta Fredricksen

AMERICA
Rosary

TO UNITE THE
I AM RACE
IN THE LINEAGE OF THE ANCIENT OF DAYS

Copyright © 2012, 2013 Alberta Fredricksen
Published by HeartPeace Now
Alberta@HeartPeaceNow.com

Publication in print sponsored in part by the Worldwide Ashram
www.WorldwideAshram.org

Cover design by Inner Artz.
Cover art: *Mary's Diamond Heart Blessing 2012* Copyright © 1999, 2012
Inner Artz. All rights reserved. www.InnerArtz.com

Editing and Layout by Diamond Heart Publishing
diamndhrt8@aol.com

First printing 2012

Congratulations!

You have just acquired two special bonuses that give you access to this book and to the special spiritual rosary ritual anywhere you go. This spiritual rosary ritual is powerful and affirming. You will have best results with this enlightening combination of information and spiritual application if you follow these steps:

Read the book or listen to the free downloadable audio version here: http://heartpeacenow.com/rosary/. This information will help you understand the spiritual sponsorship of America, the background of who and what the I AM Race is, and the power behind the rosary.

Recite the *America Rosary to Unite the I AM Race* as often as you can. You may recite the Rosary alone reading from the book. Or you may use the special audio file found here http://heartpeacenow.com/rosary/ that will allow you to offer the rosary along with other voices and enjoy musical selections. You may also play this downloadable recording in your home, car, or on your smart phone or other mobile devices to provide a spiritual force-field wherever you go.

Join us as we pray for our nation, our government and our planet! Mother Mary teaches that Love, Wisdom and Christ-awareness are the keys to restoring and reuniting the United States and all the nations. Thank you for adding your prayers to ours in support of freedom, liberty and peace for all!

Dedication

AMERICA ROSARY to Unite the I AM Race, is dedicated to Saint Germain—the Aquarian Adept of Freedom, the Blessed Mother Mary who holds the Immaculate Concept, and Jesus the Christ who shows us The Way to personal, national and planetary Christhood.

"It is a gift of the Holy Spirit to be able to interpret the events passing upon the earth and what they portend for the nations. Thus listen with the inner heart. Call forth righteous judgment. Pursue the discrimination. Pray for the nations. For God has empowered all of His people upon earth this day to deliver the prayer, the decree, and the action for world change and for the Revolution in Higher Consciousness. Accept this day as a new day of the Holy Spirit's empowerment of thy soul."[1]

—LANELLO

"Therefore, I say to you, beloved, let this be the day of your full and final declaration of independence from the fallen angels and all servants of Darkness and corruption! ...as you summon this Immaculate Concept of America that belongs to all of the I AM Race, all children of the Light of the entire world are included in the canopy of this dispensation; for the tribes come from all of the earth unto the feet of their Mighty I AM Presence. And this nation is the land consecrated to be the place where every man, [every woman,] wherever they may be, may commune with that I AM THAT I AM."[2]

—ARCHANGEL URIEL AND AURORA

Table of Contents

Part 1

Introduction to the Rosary

The rosary is one of the most cherished prayers for believers who give reverence to Mother Mary, the Mother of Jesus Christ. During this type of prayer recitation, the individual usually meditates on scriptural verses or other holy phrases that evoke the mysteries of God, the Christ of Jesus and the faithful witness of the Blessed Mother Mary.

While the origins of the rosary are a little sketchy, there are indications that this recitation of prayers, sometimes using prayer beads to aid in counting, has roots in pre-Christian times. Evidence exists from the Middle Ages that strings of beads were used to count the Lord's Prayers and the Hail Marys. The structure of the rosary gradually evolved over the centuries. Many rosaries link Hail Marys with verses, Psalms or other phrases evoking the lives of Jesus and Mary.

They allow the devotee to meditate on the mysteries of the life of Christ and implore the intercession of Mother Mary to lead believers to her Son. Other rosaries have developed over the years.

While speaking of the traditional Catholic Rosary, Archbishop Fulton Sheen said:

The rosary is the book of the blind, where souls see and there enact the greatest drama of love the world has ever known; it is the book of the simple, which initiates them into mysteries and knowledge more satisfying than the education of other men; it is the book of the aged, whose eyes close upon the shadow of this world, and open on the substance of the next. The power of the rosary is beyond description.[3]

There are a variety of formats that employ the powerful spiritual prayers of the rosary in practice today.

Dozens of 15-minute rosaries utilizing the I AM Lord's Prayer, the Hail Mary and biblical Scripture are available as "A Child's Rosary to Mother Mary," published by The Summit Lighthouse and Church Universal & Triumphant.[4] Other rosaries published include Archangel Michael's Rosary for Armageddon, Kuan Yin's Crystal Rosary with devotions to the Divine Mother East and West, the Surrender Rosary and the Enoch Rosary.[5]

Another form is called the "Patriotic Rosary for the Consecration of Our Nation," written by a Friend of Medjugorje and published by Caritas of Birmingham, a community group in Alabama where Marija, who is one of the original visionaries of Medjugorje that Mother Mary has been appearing to regularly, has received her visitations.[6]

On July 4, 2009, a very important event took place in Alabama. Marija reported that the re-consecration of America to Our Lady's Immaculate Heart was accomplished. This took place at a conference in Alabama. You can learn more at their website: http://www.medjugorje.com/medjugorje-america/medjugorje-america/658-july-4-2009-apparition-in-the-field.html

In September 1998, Elizabeth Clare Prophet, Messenger for the Great White Brotherhood[7], provided updates on the appearances of Mother Mary at Fátima and Medjugorje. These updates are published in the *Pearls of Wisdom,* Vol. 41 No. 39[8] and were delivered as part of the 40th Anniversary Celebration of the founding of The Summit Lighthouse. Mrs. Prophet said, "Mother Mary would like us to review two of the most important series of messages to have been given to lightbearers in this century—the messages from Fátima and Medjugorje...

"I believe that Mother Mary began her appearances in Medjugorje because her requests at Fátima have not been fulfilled. The pope to this day has never revealed the third part of the Fátima secret....The messages from the Blessed Mother are still being given to the visionaries. And in addition to these messages, Mother Mary has said that she will give to each of them a total of ten "secrets"—prophecies of events that will occur on earth in the near future. Mirjana, Ivanka and, most recently, Jacov, have received all ten secrets. The remaining three—Ivan, Marija and Vicka have received nine secrets..."

Mrs. Prophet shared some of Mother Mary's words to us delivered in a 1987 dictation that spoke of Mother Mary's appearances in Medjugorje:

Know, then, beloved, that I have also appeared in Yugoslavia to these special hearts, young in body but ancient of days, as the Queen of Peace. For peace is a pillar of fire that is thrust as a sword in the very midst of Communist territory... Blessed ones, Medjugorje has become as a figure-eight flow where so many hearts give attention to me that the light may descend as judgment... The simple of heart need to be reminded of their original faith. To deliver to them a message beyond that which they comprehend within the supposed security of the Church would only serve to neutralize the message and their opinions of its authenticity. Thus, to depart from scripture or canon would be to obviate the very purpose of my coming, which is to draw a tremendous devotion of people of every faith to the heart of God and the Divine Mother, that in this sacred tie to heaven they might pass through a darkness to come... I have desired, then, that you should see and understand the light, the determination, the joy, the confidence that the seeing of myself has given to the six—and which through them has been radiated to the many.

If you wish to view the messages Mother Mary is still giving to the six visionaries, visit the website displaying them: http://www.medjugorje.org/

Mrs. Prophet also said, "In response to Mother Mary, I believe it is imperative that we all give a rosary daily... I encourage you to continue giving a rosary every day in order to fulfill the Blessed Mother's request at Fatima. What a wonderful opportunity it is to spend even 15 minutes each day speaking to the Blessed Mother and turning over to her your personal burdens and the burdens of the world." I recommend her recorded rosary albums to you.[9]

America's History of Consecration to Mother Mary

The event described in Alabama on July 4, 2009 is called a *reconsecration* because there is a history of the United States of America being consecrated to Mother Mary through the Catholic Church. According to the "Our Lady of America" website link at http://jkmi.com/olashrine.asp, the following timeline illustrates this historical record:

"In 1792, the Most Reverend John Carroll of Baltimore, America's first Roman Catholic Bishop, chose the Blessed Virgin Mary as the Patroness of the United States and consecrated the newly-created nation under her protection.

"On May 13, 1846, the Bishops of the United States unanimously chose Mary, under the title of The Immaculate Conception, as the Patroness of our Land. In 1847, Pope Pius IX ratified the Bishops' action. Our Lady of America identified herself to Sister Mildred and said, 'I am the Immaculate One, Patroness of your Land.'

"All of this was reaffirmed in 1959 when the Basilica of the National Shrine of the Immaculate Conception was dedicated in Washington D.C. and the Bishops of the United States consecrated the country to her.

"Our Lady promised that the placement of her statue in the National Shrine would be a safeguard for our country, and the placement of her image or statue in the home would be a safeguard for the family... She gave a grave warning for us if we don't heed her requests.

"In April of 1957, Our Lady said, 'Unless my children reform their lives, they will suffer great persecution. If man himself will not take upon himself the penance necessary to atone for his sins and those of others, God in His justice will have to send upon him the punishment necessary to atone for his transgressions.'

"On November 22, 1980, Our Lady told Sister Mildred:

Beloved daughter, the United States is a small one among nations, yet has it not been said that 'a little child shall lead them'? It is the United States that is to lead the world to peace, the peace of Christ, the peace that He brought with Him from heaven in His birth as man in the little town of Bethlehem. Dear child, unless the United States accepts and carries out faithfully the mandate given to it by heaven to lead the world to peace, there will come upon it and all nations a great havoc of war and incredible suffering. If, however, the United States is faithful to this mandate from heaven and yet fails in the pursuit of peace because the rest of the world will not accept or co-operate, then the United States will not be burdened with the punishment about to fall.

"On November 11, 2006, the United States Bishops re-consecrated the country to the Immaculate Conception at the Basilica of the National Shrine of the Immaculate Conception" as requested by Our Lady.

And on July 4, 2009, the Medjugorje visionary, Marija, reported that the re-consecration of America to Our Lady's Immaculate Heart was accomplished in Alabama.

The Sacred Bond

*W*e find in the message below written by *A Friend of Medjugorje*, published on September 11, 2003, this same emphasis on the importance of America's victory to the victory of every nation on planet earth, of the sponsorship of our Blessed Mother Mary and the need for re-consecrating America to her Immaculate Heart every day in the Rosary.

The Sacred Bond[10]

He found a secluded spot and placed the dirt.
He wanted to make a strong foundation.
He put water on both sides. He wanted it to be hidden,
For it was a gift to his mother.

On two occasions, it would be found,*
But he managed to keep it secret until he was
ready to give it to her and then it happened. It was found.
And soon after he gave it to her who by then
Was Queen with many titles. He called it...America.

The upper part He peopled from all over the earth**
And then did the impossible,
by miraculously uniting these people of different backgrounds.
He put in their hearts an illumination,
To build a nation as the world had never seen.
Never in the history of the world
Had such a diverse group of people
Come together for such a common cause,
And though the Divine was involved,
Only the prayerful understood it.

So vivid was this vision that the original founders
Recognized clearly all was orchestrated
By the hand of Providence.
And now the veil lifts further,
To reveal that this nation's existence
From the beginning, was to be used by the Queen
for Her purposes of Peace,
consecrated to Her as Her instrument,
Her tool, to bring stability to all other lands.

A foundation to build upon, a land to bring freedom
Such as the world has never known before,
to all people of the earth.
For the prayerful, discerning heart, this is easy to see.
For the one without prayer, it is impossible to understand.
The United States of America,

12

Being consecrated to its Patroness, the Virgin Mary,
Is united to Her in a Sacred Bond
To be used for peace, as no other land
Or nation has ever been throughout all of history.

Her enemy, trying to take it away from Her,
Divided it from within,***
But She Herself came back to reclaim it
as Queen of the South.****
As gold, She now purifies it to make it one,
United, strong, shimmering from sea to sea;
America the Beautiful,
The Queen's necklace,
Her Son's rod...for peace.

America...
May God thy Gold Refine.
Till All success be nobleness, and ev'ry gain Divine.

A Friend of Medjugorje - September 11, 2003

*This refers to the fact that the land has become known as the United States of America was actually found on other occasions previous to Columbus' discovery (see "American History You Never Learned," by a Friend of Medjugorje). However, nothing came of it, for it was not time for America to be discovered by the civilized world. The first words spoken from Columbus' mouth upon seeing the land of America before him was the "Salve Regina," or the "Hail, Holy Queen."

**"The upper part" refers to "North America," as opposed to "South America."

***The author, writing "*...Her enemy, trying to take it away from Her, divided it from within...*" does not refer to the Civil War, rather it refers to the

1960s, 70s and 80s, when the foundations of our faith, our nation, and its Constitution were challenged and attacked, weakening and filling our nation with strife and division.

****The "Queen of the South" is actually referenced from both the Old and New Testaments (Luke 11:27-33; Matthew 12; 1 Kings 10; 2 Chronicles 9): *"A woman in the crowd raised her voice and said to him, "Blessed is the womb that bore you, and the breasts that you sucked!" But he said, "Blessed rather are those who hear the word of God and keep it!" When the crowds were increasing, he began to say, "This generation is an evil generation; it seeks a sign, but no sign shall be given to it except the sign of Jonah. For as Jonah became a sign to the men of Nineveh, so will the Son of man be to this generation. The queen of the South will arise at the judgment with the men of this generation and condemn them; for she came from the ends of the earth to hear the wisdom of Solomon, and behold, something greater than Solomon is here."* Luke 11:27-31. Our Lady appeared in 1988 in the south and on December 25, 1988, said, "I have come as Your Mother, Queen of Peace..." "The Queen of the South" was written into "The Sacred Bond" in reference to the apparitions in Alabama that brought with them the hope of the healing of our nation, through Our Lady reclaiming it back for God. These apparitions are the cause of the healing of our nation. It is the birthplace of renewing ourselves, families and nation back to God, through our Lady, as the Patroness of our nation.

Earth Has a Divine Plan to Become Freedom's Star

Planet earth has been referred to as a dark star for many reasons, including the warring on this planet. The Hierarchy of Light intends for earth to become Freedom's Star, and as Freedom's

Star it has a mighty role to play in this entire section of Cosmos. Lord Maitreya has promised that he "will stand with those who are determined to conquer self and conquer the dark ones in the earth and who are still determined with Saint Germain to make earth Freedom's Star!"[11]

And Saint Germain proclaims, "Lo, I AM come! Lo, I AM the defender of freedom in every heart, in every nation, and in all mankind! **Earth is destined to be a star of freedom, a star in the crown of the Cosmic Virgin!** [All bold is the author's.] And I AM the champion of that flame, that light, and of the seed, the sons and daughters of God who walk the earth...and I set my seal upon the brow of all who espouse the cause. You who will go forth in the name of freedom, claiming my flame and my momentum, which I have bequeathed not alone to America, but to all who fervently pursue the vow of unity, you who will go forth carrying that fire, will also have the momentum of my flame! For I stand this night to sponsor once again the patriarchs, the patrons, and the patriots of freedom. I sponsor those who will take the mantle and the fire and the sword. I sponsor those who reckon with the responsibility of an age."[12]

Saint Germain goes even further to show us the consequences of not bringing earth to the fulfillment of her divine plan of being Freedom's Star. "Now let us go forth as conquerors and let us slay the dragon in our midst. **For the earth must become freedom's star, for the alternative is self-annihilation. There is no middle of the road. There is no other choice but to stand for freedom or to go down into that nothingness of ignominy."[13]**

If we are to have this victory, then we earth-dwellers must unite. Beloved Omri-Tas and those of the Violet Planet who have achieved the victory of their planet through the use of the Violet Flame as given to us by Saint Germain implore us to do so. "I AM Omri-Tas, Ruler of the Violet Planet, so near to you yet so far vibrationally. O earth, that thou mayest become Freedom's Star is yet our hope, our prayer, our imploring to those Lightbearers of the world who hold the key to the seventh age. Let them unite, O God! To you we say, you who are one in heart and voice: Lightbearers of the world, unite in the name of Saint Germain!"[14]

And the Ascended Master Lanello (most recently embodied as the Messenger for the Great White Brotherhood, Mark L. Prophet) gives us instruction on how we can achieve this. "Our goal, beloved, is to see take place on earth that which is on the violet planet: 144,000 priests of the sacred fire, Masters of the violet flame, priests and priestesses...to have for each of them one lifestream upon earth who will maintain that violet flame action sufficiently to be in a figure-eight flow between that priest and that one on earth. Were this to be accomplished in this age ...that the full 144,000 candidates upon earth should be able to so sustain such a Light, it would be the beginning and the nucleus whereby that figure-eight configuration of the two planets should occur.

"The violet planet is accelerated into another vibration, higher than that of earth. And thus you see how that momentum could draw up this planet into her rightful place. **For earth's destiny [in this solar system] is to be Freedom's Star and Freedom's Star is the star of the Seventh Ray and the Seventh Age.** This is precisely the purpose of Omri-Tas' coming in Washington, D.C., many years ago, releasing [the resurgent power of the violet flame focused in the nation's Capitol and] violet flame spheres which were physically visible in the skies. It was to contact [chelas of Saint Germain and the seventh dispensation] and to increase the desire for freedom and the violet flame.

16

"You have captured those spheres, the energy thereof, in your violet flame songs and decrees... Let them increase. Let them be amplified. Let them be refined, for truly you create chalices whereby these priests of the sacred fire might find those ones, for they are known already, beloved. It is known in the cosmic computer of the Mind of God who upon earth are those [144,000] who could attain to that level. Think of it, beloved. And some of them include these unascended masters who desire to come into embodiment for this very purpose."15

Saint Germain's twin flame of freedom declares, "I, Portia, am here by my love of Saint Germain. May you also be here with me for that very same love. There is no greater love, for through his heart is the Light and Life of the seventh dispensation.

"May it [the seventh dispensation] not be lost to ages of darkness and war and plague and death as has been a major portion of the age of Pisces. But let this age truly be seen as the sign of the turning around of universes, systems of worlds and individuals because...that last measure of violet flame was invoked and finally—their burden removed by the simple act of devotion of a single son or daughter maintaining the flame...that one individual and that one times a billion could leap and come to his senses and awake! and awake! and awake and be, then, once again the living flame that he was in the beginning with God with twin flame in the Central Sun... I am...the Mother of Aquarius. Call to me, for I am Portia and I have stepped down from cosmic levels to be with you. **As you receive me, earth shall become Freedom's Star."**16

Even more astounding and magnificent, is this amazing revelation about the earth's role among the planets! The mighty Elohim of the Third Ray of Love tell us, "Sons and daughters of the flame, be one in our love and let this flow of fire melt with a fervent heat the elements in all of the planes of Mater. So let that melting be a consuming of all pollution of the etheric plane, the mental plane, the emotional quadrant, and the physical earth. So let this love be for the transforming, healing action of Terra as Terra herself is ordained as a minister of the sacred fire among the planets and planetary homes. So let the earth be freedom's star to show all evolutions what freedom is."[17]

And the Ancient of Days, Sanat Kumara himself reveals that "Venus, the planet of love, is the heart chakra of the solar system, representing the heart of Helios and Vesta in the planets who focus the light of the seven rays. As earth is freedom's star, representing the soul of all evolutions, so she has played host to all lifewaves of this system of worlds, for solar consciousness is the destiny of the beings of earth—freedom through solar awareness."[18]

America Is the Key in God's Plan for Earth's Victory

*W*ithin the family of nations that comprise the earth today, each nation represents a part of the body of God, and each one has a special role to play in the victory of earth as Freedom's Star. The United States of America, or America, is the model nation sponsored by the Great White Brotherhood.

Other researchers such as Peter Marshall and David Manuel also reached similar conclusions about America's role as a covenanted or sponsored nation. They wrote, "Did God have a plan for America? Many have discovered the reality of the living

Christ, and pursued the belief that God has a plan for each individual's life—a plan that could, with spiritual effort, be discerned and followed.

"What if He dealt with whole nations in the same way? The Bible said He did..." And a lot of other individuals, sacred texts and spiritual teachings also teach this as a part of our history on planet Earth.[19]

In Columbus' time, the lands that encompass America were called the New World, even as we now long to establish the Ascended Masters' version of a New World Order of the Ages. Not the New World Order as the fallen ones have contrived it and as they are scheming even now to enslave all the peoples of the world. But the *New World Order of the Ages* which is the result of the Revolution of Higher Consciousness - where a greater percentage of mankind can walk and talk with the angels, masters and cosmic beings.

Now we are the *New Age* discoverers as Columbus was the New World discoverer. All of us are here now on a rescue mission. No matter what country we are living in or where we were born, it's about the mission to planet Earth in which we are a part. And the Great Divine Director, the teacher or Guru of Saint Germain, told us that America is the heart of the Great White Brotherhood's action in the world.[20] And he also said that all nations are intended to gravitate to their rightful "place in the sun" where the reality of Cosmic Law can be taught.

So this is a KEY to this great mission. Where on the planet earth are people free enough to pursue the teachings of the God Reality of Cosmic Law? Where is there enough right abundance that allows the time and resources to be invested in study, worship and a pursuit of happiness in Spirit?

It is America! The very letters of the name of this nation are the same letters that spell the words of the "I AM Race!"

This nation has been blessed and it is surely sponsored. Our responsibility to this sponsorship is great, for "to whom much is given, much is expected."[21]

The Spiritual Sponsorship of America

*I*n 1959, Saint Germain instructed us saying, "Truly, America was designed from our octave and given so much assistance from there to be 'the land of the free...!' Now, every nation and its people are dear to our hearts—for all are some expression of God's Life and His Life is the only Life there is. Each nation has a divine plan of its own to fulfill and, according to their divine destinies, the various nations of the world represent the various parts of the earth's body. Therefore, in the new age, the land of India shall represent the 'head' of such an 'earth body' and the land of America the 'heart.' Take notice, please, that the name 'India' begins with the letter 'I' and 'America' with 'Am.' Is this not significant?

"The land of America—in the main so little understood by most of the dear lifestreams she shelters—is of far more importance to all life on this planet than most imagine. America is a land somewhat different from others—for she has gathered to her bosom many from every land who love freedom. Since that particular virtue is the one I personally embody (and is my reason for being), these individuals are particularly dear to my heart. Is not America considered to be 'the melting pot' of the world?

"You will remember the words 'Conceived in Liberty....' which appear in the 'Gettysburg Address' spoken so eloquently by the beloved Abraham Lincoln nearly a century ago. Privileged was I to have inspired the words of that address. Therefore, designed from our octave also was the idea of placing the great Statue of Liberty in New York Harbor—that open door to your great land. The radiating light and flame of divine love from the gracious Goddess of Liberty through that statue (whose 'likeness' it is) is a much more powerful protection to your Eastern seaboard and entire nation than any unascended being has any idea.

"Eternal vigilance is the price of liberty! Therefore, a strong and grateful love for one's country (not only his native land but also for his 'adopted' nation) and a fervently determined desire to have them well-governed and invincibly protected at all times should not be considered as belonging only to a specified few who are able to dedicate their entire time and energies thereto. Our loyal chelas will do all they can to this end...and like calls should also go forth from every beating heart who lives, moves and has his (or her) being within the spacious borders of this dear land..."[22]

On another occasion in 1977, Saint Germain said, "We would like to expand today in the consciousness not only of those presently assembled here, but also in those assembled in the entire community of the United States and the world an awareness of the oneness of life upon the planet that we may be able to create in America in the future that Holy-Family concept that will draw mankind together and set before the people of this planet a cup of light in the heart of America."[23]

"America's place in the destiny of the cosmos comes to the fore under the influence of the hierarch of Aquarius. **It is the place where the cosmic Virgin enshrines the flame of freedom not in temples made with hands, but upon the altar of the hearts of a people.** Drawn from every nation, from every lifewave and evolution, the American people are chosen as the standard-bearers of an age—not by the favoritism of an anthropomorphic god, but by the choice of a free will God-ordained. The elect of the Lord are those who elect to be instruments of the Lord.

"And so America is the Motherland come again. Founded by the Brotherhood on the matrix of the original thirteen of Christ and his apostles, it is the fulfillment of the destinies of the peoples of Lemuria and Atlantis, of ancient Greece and Rome, of the golden ages of China and India, of Egypt and Europe. To America the pilgrims of freedom have marched. Over four centuries they have journeyed to the place prepared in the wilderness for the coming of the Woman clothed with the Sun and birth of her Divine Manchild...

"By unseen hand and the very specific guidance of the ascended masters, America—the heart, the mind, the soul of a world—was born. America is the place of the rise of the feminine potential of man and woman. It is the place of creativity—aspiration and inspiration engendering the rise of God consciousness in all. It is the place where freedom of religion, freedom of speech, freedom of the press, and freedom to assemble provide the foundation for the individual pursuit of cosmic consciousness...

"America was founded by the ascended masters as a place secure, protected—a land of abundant resources and opportunity, a land where the forum of the greatest souls of the ages would one day produce the greatest science and the greatest religion of all time and space.

"**In order for the soul to attain cosmic consciousness, it must become the Mother.** Where there is life, where there is joy, where there is self-discipline in creativity, where there is love and freedom, there is the Mother ray activating the soul to self-awareness. There is the Mother ray giving birth to the Christ and the Buddha that is the real identity of every man, woman and child.

"America is an experiment of the Great White Brotherhood. No psychological or astrological predictions determine her fate. There is nothing automatic about the fulfillment of a cosmic destiny. America is simply opportunity, the gift of freedom, like the gift of free will, in the hands and the hearts of a peculiar people. If indeed there is to be a cosmic destiny forged and won on this continent, it will be because this people have made the work of the ages their own."[24]

Before America was a nation, she was an inspiration—in the heart and mind of a visionary explorer. This is what Christopher Columbus himself wrote about how he came to the Americas.

> It was the Lord who put into my mind (I could feel his hand upon me) the fact that it would be possible to sail from here to the Indies. All who heard of my project rejected it with laughter, ridiculing me. There is no question that the inspiration was from the Holy Spirit, because He comforted me with rays of marvelous inspiration from the Holy Scriptures...
>
> I am a most unworthy sinner, but I have cried out to the Lord for grace and mercy, and they have covered me completely. I have found the sweetest consolation since I made it my whole purpose to enjoy His marvelous presence. For the

execution of the journey to the Indies, I did not make use of intelligence, mathematics or maps. It is simply the fulfillment of what Isaiah had prophesied...

No one should fear to undertake any task in the name of our Savior, if it is just and if the intention is purely for His holy service. The working out of all things has been assigned to each person by our Lord, but it all happens according to His sovereign will, even though He gives advice. He lacks nothing that it is in the power of men to give Him. Oh, what a gracious Lord, who desires that people should perform for Him those things for which He holds Himself responsible! Day and night, moment by moment, everyone should express their most devoted gratitude to Him.[25]

Now some might say that Columbus simply discovered the New World by accident while seeking a trade route to the Indies. From our current vantage point in the historical cycles of the I AM Race, we know that the Ascended Master Saint Germain was previously embodied as Christopher Columbus and that every individual soul's dharma or ultimate mission develops over the embodiments that he or she has lived. What is interesting to note is that even in that lifetime, Columbus felt he had been given his life's mission directly by God...that he felt called to bear the Light of Christ to undiscovered lands in fulfillment of prophetic passages in the Bible and that he knew he had been guided by the Holy Spirit the whole way.

Peter Marshall and David Manuel ask the questions: "What if Columbus's discovery had not been accidental at all? What if it was merely the opening curtain of an extraordinary drama?" Haven't the first settlers described themselves as "having been called by God to found a new nation based on the centrality of the Christian faith and God's Word?"[26]

The aspirations that drove the immigrants and settlers to journey to the New World and the intentions and firm belief held by the founders in the guidance of Divine Providence behind the subsequent establishment of this nation have been amply recorded in monuments, writings, letters and sermons throughout that period of time.

Dr. Peter Marshall (the senior) taught that "A covenant nation is one which recognizes God and His purposes stand about the nation and the nation's interests, and that the highest role a nation can play is to reflect God's righteousness in national policy. Ours, therefore, is a covenant nation—covenanted with God in the beginning.

"This country was founded in religious faith. It had different expressions, to be sure — Quakers, Puritans, Congregationalists, Presbyterians, Anglicans, Methodists, and Baptists, Lutherans, and Catholics of French, Spanish, and Irish stock....

"They founded schools that were rooted in religion — Harvard and Yale were founded by Congregationalists; the Universities of Columbia and Pennsylvania by Episcopalians; Princeton by Presbyterians; Duke and Northwestern by Methodists; the University of Chicago by Baptists; Fordham and Notre Dame by Roman Catholics."[27]

Since the very inception of America, this nation has been targeted by the fallen ones and their councils of darkness to prevent the development of the Christ consciousness among the people. From the beginning to the present hour, they have backed candidates of all political parties and manipulated the educational systems and media to move us away from the founding principles and values that were God-centered. They pervert freedom of religion into anti-religion; glorify the accumulation of power, wealth and control; and dismiss personal immorality as symbols of success and privilege. The right to life, sanctity of marriage, the cultural keystone of the family, and personal responsibility are being displaced by the death culture, selfishness, greed and government regulations over God and man.

The Ten Commandments so carefully carved into our monuments and engrafted in our legal system are being challenged and thrown out of courthouses. Those who instruct or quote scripture, or speak of sin against God or against mankind are labeled guilty of hate crimes. And they have sought the total annihilation of the economies of the people, both as individuals and as nations, with the intent to enslave them. The people are divided on many key issues including language, culture, decency and even the motivations behind deploying military forces to other nations. Are they sent to defend freedom in other nations who know not how to defend it or are they sent to secure resources for the worldwide power elite who act on behalf of the dark forces to control the people and set man against man?

We have an obligation to choose leaders wisely and also to be leaders that are God-centered. We have an obligation to seek truth, to expose truth and to be truth in action. I recently read a small book by Andy Andrews, titled *How Do You Kill 11 MILLION PEOPLE? Why the truth Matters More than You Think.* Now the short answer to that question is that you lie to them. You lie to them! "The only way we have to know a person who aspires to lead us is to listen to what he says and watch what he does. Frankly, what *I* might think of any current or past leader of the United States should be irrelevant to you. The questions most important in your life in regard to this subject should be: What criteria do you use to determine who leads your family?

And what do *you* think?"[28] What criteria do *you* use to determine who and what leads you in your personal path; who leads your family, your church, your city government, state and nation?

"If the truth is what sets us free, what does it mean to live in a society where truth is absent? How do truth and lies in the past shape our destiny today? Through the lens of the Holocaust, Andy Andrews examines the critical need for truth in our relationships, our communities, and our government."[29]

Saint Germain has explained to us why it is more difficult to have sound policy in a representative form of a Republic as we have in America. When you have a large Congress with many voices, many changes, and much deliberation and confusion, it is more difficult than working with just one office where the power of the Godhead could be directed to the people, monitored, and held in balance by the presence of the prophet among the people. But with all these many voices, achieving unity is more difficult.[30]

"These individuals have positioned themselves to the right, to the left, and in the middle of the entire political and economic spectrum. So we must understand how the seed of Light, the seed of Christ, and the tares sown among the good seed are now intertwined karmically in many situations upon earth—a sprinkling of the sons of God and many of the fallen ones occupying seats of power in all fields."[31]

He said that though the Masters "are able to use all to deliver our Word from time to time, it is *the consistency*, it is *the constancy* of the Keeper of the Flame of Freedom that is necessary for a continuing direction for the charting of the voyage of discovery into the new age—for the voyage of the ship of state."[32]

Today, in 2012, America is a nation divided, and a nation divided cannot stand. Indeed, America as a nation is on the cross.

Jesus submitted to the initiation of the crucifixion on the path leading to personal Christhood and the ascension. It is The Way that he has shown for us as students on the path of the ascension. And so it is also for nations. We know that America cannot get to the resurrection and the ascension without going through the crucifixion.

In 1973, Mother Mary said: "We see that the crucifixion of America is nigh. We see that the crucifixion of the Feminine Ray has come, and mankind are not ready for the triumph. And those who are not ready shall perish, precious hearts."[33] Many parts and peoples of the earth have experienced and will continue to experience the crucifixion. And we pray for all nations.

However, in 1992, nineteen years after Mother Mary's statement above, the Buddha of the Ruby Ray said: "Yes, there is that joining with the hosts of the Lord, the mighty Archangels, for the rescue of many and many parts of the world! This is a time, however, when you must concentrate on America itself as the United States and America, North and South, comprising the entire hemisphere. For this is an hour, beloved, of great trial and crucifixion in these fifty states."[34]

With all of this division, it becomes more and more difficult for America to manifest the model nation of freedom and liberty, to welcome all as the melting pot of the world and still protect her borders, and to still send her treasure and her blood to the rescue of peoples and nations around this entire planetary body without falling prey to the vicious energy that is "hatred of America."

This hatred of America is hatred of the Light, hatred of the Christ consciousness, hatred of the platform where one is free enough to be able and allowed to rise in consciousness. And it is hatred of the heart capacity to care about the rest of the world and the souls that she represents. America's victory to fulfill her divine plan is not preordained. It is a grand experiment of the Brotherhood and the outcome is not certain.

El Morya said, "We are not separatists regarding America. We say that this is the place of the experiment of the Great White Brotherhood and of the endowment of Saint Germain. **We say that if the experiment fails here, it will not succeed anywhere else.** For the peculiar people of ancient Atlantis and even Lemuria have reincarnated here to take up where they left off and to finish the work begun.

"Thus, America is more than a nation. It is yet a symbol to all people of the (ongoing) possibility for the realization of individual and world freedom. [The realization of this possibility] therefore rests upon the shoulders of those who have known freedom in the past, those who have embraced it and realized the expansion of the flame of Liberty in the heart."[35]

The Ascended Master El Morya described the valor and courage of men like General George Washington, who declined to be King and was America's first President, and he said that those days of the early American patriots "were the days when there did surely hang in the balance the entire blueprint for America. **And that blueprint is yet there, overlaid upon the fifty states and more, overlaid upon the I AM Race residing in many nations.** Much has come between the blueprint and that which [should have manifested] in the earth, much that must be righted. Yet it can be righted, for Saint Germain has released the dispensation of the golden age of Aquarius and our Mother Liberty stands tall in this hour—stands tall, beloved, to enfire every heart with its own mission... Let the voice of America return to one voice, one sound of the will of God! Let the people of America come together in the reality of cosmic history and not a history revised."[36]

Elizabeth Clare Prophet said, "When Guy Ballard was embodied as George Washington, Saint Germain anointed him our first president. In this century the Master called upon him to reembody and to work with the American people, this time to give them the knowledge of the I AM Presence and of themselves as the "I AM" Race. The I AM Race is composed of citizens of all nations who have the I AM Presence and the divine spark within them. So the one whom we know today as the Ascended Master Godfre returned in this century to deliver to us the missing link to our spiritual identity and to our placing the capstone on the pyramid of our civilization."[37] And as the Messenger, Mrs. Prophet has stumped the nations to bring that message to those of the I AM Race everywhere.

Who and What Is the I AM Race?

The I AM Race are lightbearers having descended from above with the Presence of the I AM THAT I AM. They form a mandala of souls from every race and every nation who are called Americans because in a metaphysical sense, the word America is composed of the seven letters that spell I AM Race. This mandala consists of the twelve tribes and the 144,000 of the lightbearers and the sons of God who are to ascend in this age.[38]

Saint Germain describes the I AM Race as "those who are the descendants of Lord Sanat Kumara. Let us understand that the seed of light, the Christic seed descended from on high, are those which have this I AM Presence of the Lord God."

He said, "Many years ago I called my minutemen and women in the service of the Great I AM to the upholding of the cosmic honor flame in the heart of America—that promised land unto the chosen ones who are of the I AM Race.

"What is the I AM Race? It is an evolution of lightbearers who have not lost the memory of their God consciousness nor of the person of the Ancient of Days. Though some of these have gone astray of the path of initiation under Sanat Kumara, yet one and all retain the inner memory of the individualization of the Godhead identified to Moses in Horeb as Jehovah, the God of Israel, the self-proclaimed I AM WHO I AM. This teaching and this dispensation are for the quickening of the soul's memory of the I AM Presence in those men and women who are called upon to hold the balance of the age."[39]

Immigrants to America Bear Witness

*M*rs. Prophet recommended that we read about the life of Dr. Peter Marshall—that immigrant patriot who came to America from Scotland and rose to be the chaplain to the United States Senate and to minister to the people of Washington D.C. and America, especially in a time of world war.

In a collection of war time sermons by Dr. Marshall, one sermon is titled *The Covenant Nation.* "The forces of evil are organized on a world scale. They fight against God, against religion, against peace. They seek to promote confusion, to sow suspicion, and to set man against man. All who believe in God, who love America, who cherish our heritage, who seek peace, who are sick of war, and who long for goodness, must fight for these things—and they are worth fighting for."[40]

"Ours is a covenant nation...the only surviving nation on earth, I believe, that had its origins in the determination of the Pilgrim Fathers to establish on this continent a settlement 'to the glory of God and the advancement of the Christian faith.'

"God seems to have placed America in a position where she can lead the nations of the world into a new world order—of international justice, ethics, and righteousness...or...by our hypocrisy, our compromises, our expediencies...and our own immorality, sow the seeds of cynicism and disillusionment from which this nation shall never recover in a hundred years..."[41]

Dr. Peter Marshall quoted a fighting man, John J. Hogan, who wrote home to his parents during WWI: "The men who fought for victory will now have to fight for peace. God knows these men fought for America... But that was not enough. They, and we—all of us—must now fight for the peace, for the peace of the world. That is the challenge that faces America today."

Dr. Marshall continued in his sermon saying, "Peace is a fruit of righteousness. How then can there be peace anywhere in the world until there is righteousness among the nations? How can there be peace in any human heart where there is wrong thinking and wrong living?...

"The plain fact is that there can be no peace where there is no righteousness. The Bible has been telling us that for centuries. Our own consciences tell us the same thing. That is God's truth."[41]

Rev. Heinrich Richard Wurmbrand, a Romanian Evangelical Christian Minister, was imprisoned and brutally tortured for fourteen years and has been called "the Voice of the Underground Church" and the "Iron Curtain Paul." The Ascended Master El Morya said, "We look here and there over the face of the earth and truly we declare that those isolated individuals such as Reverend

Wurmbrand who are determined tell the true story of torture and torment of Christians—these are they whose voice of Truth will never be denied. The flame of freedom cannot be put out! It speaks in many, many hearts."[43]

Rev. Wurmbrand demonstrated that internal Flame of Freedom in the heart—and he articulated his thoughts about America and her role in this world, saying: "Every freedom-loving man has two fatherlands; his own and America. Today, America is the hope of every enslaved man, because it is the last bastion of freedom in the world. Only America has the power and spiritual resources to stand as a barrier between militant Communism and the people of the world.

"It is the last 'dike' holding back the rampaging flood waters of militant Communism. If it crumples, there is no other dike, no other dam; no other line of defense to fall back upon.

"America is the last hope of millions of enslaved peoples. They look to it as their second fatherland. In it lies their hopes and prayers.

"I have seen fellow-prisoners in Communist prisons beaten, tortured, with 50 pounds of chains on their legs—praying for America that the dike will not crumple; that it will remain free."[44]

The Heavenly Hosts Bear Witness

SAINT GERMAIN: "In my final life as Francis Bacon I endeavored to set forth, as I was able, those keys to the destiny of America that each and every one of you hold, as members of the I AM Race, within the nucleus of your heart in a very precious golden box that is upon the altar of your temple. There, in the heart of Life, are the secrets of the ages and the mysteries which I have come to unveil. I AM indeed the one anointed as the seventh angel in this dispensation, come for the finishing of the mystery of God! Blessed ones, the unveiling of those mysteries through beloved Godfre and Lotus and through your own messengers has come to an hour of fulfillment for many—and to the hour of beginning for others among you."[45]

ARCHANGEL URIEL: "Let us speak, then, of the good karma of this I AM Race—these 'Americans.' Let us speak, then, of the good works done in recent centuries and in many lifetimes of the past. Thus be it known that the glory of life and the very sponsorship of Jesus Christ and Saint Germain of this nation to be a place of Christed ones does descend from ancient times and is manifest through your very own sacred labor.

"Understand the equation, then. You have light in your causal body, yet someone else would take this light and squander it. It is as though you had an inheritance and knew not of it and suddenly found one day that you had had this inheritance, but before its discovery thieves came in and stole it from you and you were bereft of it.

"So it is in this age of the sons and daughters of God who descended to earth to serve as wayshowers to the people. A spiritual inheritance is thine. Many today have squandered their material inheritance for a number of reasons. But, blessed ones, do you see that it is truly because of your good karma that you ought to be and should be protected in this age for a spiritual path leading unto a golden age that even the Ascended Masters and heavenly hosts have prepared, beginning as a nucleus in this nation and spiraling to incorporate the entire earth?

"Thus, beloved, that which is deserved, that which is earned sometimes goes unclaimed, undefended. And this is exactly the situation you find yourselves in today. Because it is decreed that spiritual and physical defense is yours (decreed by Almighty God and your previous good works), you must therefore defend that inheritance and defend that divine decree and affirm it yourselves. You must fight for your right to be. Every world savior or savior nation that has done so has endured to extend the blessings of its civilization to all other nations."[46]

GAUTAMA BUDDHA: "This is the land, America. To us it is a miracle, 'a miracle of life.' It is that inner key to the fulfillment of all miracles and dreams and hopes of liberty. America—a miracle of the I AM Race....It is the golden eagle of America. It is the symbol of redemption. And so the gathering together of the eagles is the great gathering of those who are called and have been called of old for this hour of the victory."[47]

LORD MAITREYA: "O America, I, Maitreya, call to you today! I call to the souls of the good people, the God people. **Rise to the level of the Sacred Heart of your Jesus Christ! Rise to the Immaculate Heart of your most beloved Mother Mary! Rise to the Immaculate Heart! Rise to the Immaculate Heart! Rise to her heart and love her, for she does contain in that heart the divine resolution for this nation and every nation under God.**

"**And when I say I will restore America to her Christhood, I am speaking of America as the I AM Race and [I am speaking of] the I AM Race embodied in every nation, in every race, in every area of the planet.*** I come to restore that Christhood in you who have let it go down. And some of you have let it go down to the very ground and you have lost that

Light." [*The word America is composed of seven letters, which form the words I AM Race. The term 'I AM Race' refers collectively to a group of souls from all nations who have one thing in common: they all have an I AM Presence and threefold flame.][48]

ARCHANGEL MICHAEL: "Though you may know it not, you have a specific need for my services. And I offer them gladly, as I position myself in the very midst of the mounting spiral of the eighties and certain conditions which have begun on earth and which have been begun by certain individuals who are not of the Light.

"Following the natural course of these spirals, then, there has been projected upon the screen of this decade, war as well as rumors of war—some coming to pass and some fizzling, as you would say. I underscore for you, beloved hearts of light, that never has the need been greater for the protection of America, for the seed of the I AM Race, for each and every individual lightbearer in every nation, on every continent, in the sea and under the sea!"[49]

Three Prophecies

*A*rchangel Zadkiel's Prophecy – In March 1996, Archangel Zadkiel delivered a dictation in South America where the Messenger Elizabeth Clare Prophet was stumping to prepare the people of that continent regarding their sponsorship in the lineage of Sanat Kumara, the Ancient of Days. On this occasion, Zadkiel reviewed part of a previous message that he called "a pivotal dictation" he delivered on November 25, 1987 in Washington, D.C.

"In this dictation, I laid before the people of America, Keepers of the Flame and stalwart sons and daughters of God two options for the future. I painted two scenes: a scene of victory and a scene of defeat for the United States and, consequently, for planet earth. I stated that the lightbearers must determine which way the planet would go. My message applied not only to the citizens of the United States of America but to the citizens of the entire Western Hemisphere. Following is an excerpt of that dictation:

I cast before you now a vision of violet flame, as over the land a sacred fire does burn: all of America covered by violet flame. This is the vision whereby you see what destiny America can deliver unto the nations. It is a future of hope, prosperity and light, and an inner walk with God. This is the vision of Saint Germain....

This is Option the First whereby you the Lightbearers, by Holy Amethyst's ray, determine that the all-consuming fire of God shall be for transmutation and transformation in the earth body and element, in the sea and the waters, and in the air....

The scene of violet flame covering the land is one that can be accomplished by you. And if it is not, beloved, then you will see Option the Second. You will see coming to pass the third vision of George Washington:

You will see a cloud coming forth out of the east and out of the West and over the seas. You will see warfare and bloodshed upon this very continent and soil. You will see, beloved, cities of the nation overcome and burdened, a people rising up by the call of Micah, the Angel of Unity, to be one and to turn back the Adversary. And you will see as hope against hope the failing of those of America to turn back that nightmare of the Great War.

"You will see, then, that the only deliverance that can come to a people so unprepared as this to face a world war is Divine Intervention. And yet, beloved, though the angelic host descend, some among you must be pillars of fire whereby to anchor that Divine Intercession.

"Therefore, see and know, beloved, that what kind of victory shall be your own is truly your choice and choosing in this hour."[50]

George Washington's Third Vision – In 1988, Elizabeth Clare Prophet said, "Saint Germain has given to us a vision of America and so has the Archangel Zadkiel. But two centuries ago the Goddess of Liberty gave a vision to George Washington. We are all familiar with it but it is well to allow the cadences of the mind to move across these words... We see the three episodes in America's history foretold in George Washington's vision as the opportunity to balance the karma of the misuse of the threefold flame and to restore the destiny and path of our personal Christhood and America's Christhood."[51]

You can read the entire vision in multiple places on the Internet. Only the third episode is included here, as originally told by Anthony Sherman who reported that he was at Valley Forge during the winter of 1777-78, and his story was first published in an article in the *National Tribune*, 1880.

And again I heard the mysterious voice saying, "Son of the Republic, look and learn." At this the dark shadowy angel placed a trumpet to his mouth and blew three distinct blasts; and taking water from the ocean, he sprinkled it upon Europe, Asia and Africa. Then my eyes beheld a fearful scene: From each of these countries arose thick, black clouds that were soon joined into one. Throughout this mass there gleamed a dark red light by which I saw hordes of armed men, who, moving with the cloud, marched by land and sailed by sea to America. Our country was enveloped in this volume of cloud, and I saw these vast armies devastate the whole country and burn the villages, town, and cities that I beheld springing up. As my ears listened to the thundering of the cannon, clashing of sword, and the shouts and cries of millions in mortal combat, I heard again the mysterious voice saying, "Son of the Republic, look and learn." When the voice had ceased, the dark shadowy angel placed his trumpet once more to his mouth, and blew a long and fearful blast. Instantly a light as of a thousand suns shone down from above me, and pierced and broke into fragments the dark cloud which enveloped America. At the same moment the angel upon whose head still shone the word Union, and who bore our national flag in one hand and a sword in the other, descended from the heavens attended by legions of white spirits. These immediately joined the inhabitants of America, who I perceived were will nigh overcome, but who immediately taking courage again, closed up their broken ranks and renewed the battle.

Again, amid the fearful noise of the conflict, I heard the mysterious voice saying, "Son of the Republic, look and learn." As the voice ceased, the shadowy angel for the last time dipped water from the ocean and sprinkled it upon America. Instantly the dark cloud rolled back, together with the armies it had brought, leaving the inhabitants of the land victorious!

Then once more, I beheld the villages, towns and cities springing up where I had seen them before, while the bright angel, planting the azure standard he had brought in the midst of them, cried with a loud voice: "While the stars remain, and the heavens send down dew upon the earth, so long shall the Union last." And taking from his brow the crown on which blazoned the word

"Union," he placed it upon the Standard while the people, kneeling down, said, "Amen."

The scene instantly began to fade and dissolve, and I at last saw nothing but the rising, curling vapor I at first beheld. This also disappearing, I found myself once more gazing upon the mysterious visitor, who, in the same voice I had heard before, said, "Son of the Republic, what you have seen is thus interpreted: Three great perils will come upon the Republic. The most fearful is the third, but in this greatest conflict the whole world united shall not prevail against her. Let every child of the Republic learn to live for his God, his land and the Union." With these words the vision vanished, and I started from my seat and felt that I had seen a vision wherein had been shown to me the birth, progress, and destiny of the United States.

Saint Germain's Prophecy – Saint Germain has prophesied, "Here is the crossroads of Absolute Evil of the galaxies. Here on planet earth. **I tell you, beloved, angels attend as the words come out of your mouths. No sooner is the decree released than bands of angels rush forward to fulfill the fiat. This is an age of a technological war in the physical octave...those who win this battle cannot win it without reinforcement of spiritual fire, night and day, by those who understand the science of the spoken Word...**

"The victory may be projected by the LORD God. But the outcome is not known until the victors fight the good fight and win. You have seen what it has taken in decree power, hour after hour, to achieve your ends and our goals. May you equate that in an understanding of what it will take to endow the forces of Light of America and the West to defeat a very determined, ruthless, inhuman enemy. If the third vision come to pass because men have not heeded my call...**if there should be war upon this soil, it will be turned back only by divine intervention. This is the prophecy, beloved ones.**

"Where do you suppose this divine intervention will come from? Yea, <u>you must be the answer to that prayer</u> and, by the power of God, sustain heaven on earth in that Inner Retreat while a nation groans to regain a freedom and a purity and a standard that they allowed to be dragged through the streets.

"**Be fearless, beloved, but be watchful. Be bold, but decree.**"[52]

The reason for reviewing these prophecies and vision is to compel us to truly understand and comprehend that **America must be covered by a sea of violet flame and that only our unity in invoking divine intercession will prevail in overcoming the forces of darkness.**

Unity Is Required to Place the Capstone on the Pyramid

The Elohim Cyclopea and Sanat Kumara instruct about the meaning and symbology of the Great Pyramid and the missing capstone to the worldwide Community of the Great White Brotherhood.

"Why do you suppose then that the capstone is missing? It is because, very simply, **there has never manifested in this octave a body of souls unascended who could make that pledge of eternal unity, of fusion! Thus the pyramid remains without its capstone and humanity without the light to guide them.**"[53]

What comprises the capstone? "The capstone then as the all-seeing Eye of God that shall not be removed from the Earth is... composed of the initiates of the sacred fire... These initiates, each one placing upon the altar the white cube of the heart, provide the building blocks of that mighty capstone. Because these initiates have a more than ordinary oneness than all others who have built the pyramid from the foundation to its present manifestation, therefore in the manifestation of the capstone their white cubes become as one single stone, one single capstone. This is the mystery of the capstone—that it can never be taken apart. Though it is composed of many stones, these by the alchemy of the Great God become one single stone to hold the all-seeing Eye of God..."[54]

Unity is everything! This is the instruction from Micah, Angel of Unity. "Therefore let unity prevail among all Keepers of the Flame throughout the world, throughout your focuses all over the continents. So let unity be the byword of those who have found the original matrix of Christhood within their hearts....a house divided will not stand! It never has stood and it never will stand... There is absolutely no looking back. You can only look forward to a golden future and hopefully a golden age. And hopefully by that time you have merged yourself with the cause of Saint Germain and Portia and all beings of the seventh ray. And if you will come to that place and leave all else behind you and cast it into the violet flame, then you have an opportunity to make your ascension in this life."[55]

We must have more violet flame and more unity. "When all of you are one, when all of you have put into the flame your divisions and all divisiveness, when all of you can...follow your Lord and Saviour unto the ritual of your ascension...Heaven will be there! We will be there in full force.

"And there are some among you here that have a number of years to go (some lesser, some greater), but time is moving on and time is not in your favor. Therefore, *seize* the moment! ...Go after that world transmutation. Mitigate the potential of war, a third world war or a third Antichrist."[56]

"America, India, all nations must reach out through the hearts of their people to know the full meaning of liberation and freedom from falsely imposed materialistic bondage—from the old habits of greed and tyranny of the centuries and the round of senseless inharmonies which have but wearied the hearts of mankind without bringing peace to any man. The Christ sought to erect no tabernacle save the House of Peace within men. He sought the Unity of each heart with its Divine Presence, and the unity of understanding between heart and heart. His is the way of Peace and hence free from all destruction."[57]

A Planetary Assignment for the I AM Race

*I*n 1973, Saint Germain implored us saying, "Now will you give your all and make this the greatest victory of the Golden Age culture that the world has ever known, that America has ever known, that mankind has ever seen—that America might stand, and stand fast, through all of the crucifixion and the darkness that is upon her and comfort as the greatest domain of Lightbearers who then shall go forth with the true teaching of the Law to every nation and kindred, every people and every tongue, setting forth the true teaching of The Everlasting Gospel that shall raise all into the Christ Consciousness and ultimately the planetary body into the ascension itself."[58]

The cosmic being, Mighty Victory, summarized: "Precious hearts, as a nation, **America is destined to be the great example of victory. As Jesus Christ was the avatar for the Piscean age, so America is the pilot nation selected by the Ascended Masters.** [Here] people of every race, nationality and creed may merge their energies, their very blood in the melting pot so that the threefold flame of Christ light may come forth in balanced manifestation, so that the Constitution of America, written by Saint Germain as a divine document, might find parallel in the constitution of all nations upon earth.

"Precious hearts, ponder well that **it is not America, her government or her people who are at fault. It is the infiltration of the fallen ones, the dark ones and their systems of chaos and disintegration, their failure to pass the test of the ten, their abuse of capitalistic society by the laggard consciousness of greed, their failure to uphold the Christ as the head of every business, every government, every household.**

"Thus America must return to the feet of our God. Americans en masse must unite to preserve the flame of freedom. Right or wrong. That which is unreal can be consumed; that which is real can be set on high as a goal, as an ensign for all nations and all peoples....

"**Renew your fervor and dedication to the flame that is the reality of America.** We do not ask you to dedicate yourselves to the corrupt ones who corrupt others, to their flaws, failures or to darkness. Nay, **we ask you to dedicate yourselves to the principles of the victory of the Christ light in this people who yet retain** to this very hour the greatest light and the greatest love of any people upon the globe. And I say this as my analysis from inner levels.

"Believe it and know that the potential for victory for the entire planet is here. Do not flee America as rats fleeing a sinking ship. Some have done this, retreating to other countries, other places where they felt the economic climate was better.

"This is the time to plant your feet firmly on the soil of America, to let the hierarchies of light channel their energies through you to hold the balance in the hour of Libra when the hierarchies of Victory stand in the flame of the Holy Spirit that is the flame of the golden west.

"America is the fulfillment of the flame of the Holy Spirit in the Western Hemisphere. The Northern and Southern Hemispheres [of America] must be united and serve together with the understanding of the threefold flame as power, wisdom and love so that the seventh root race might be born, that the archetypes of freedom might be etched in fire for the victory of an age—the Aquarian age of the lightbearers.

"We lead with the flame of Victory!"[59]

Call to Action

*F*riends of Freedom of all nations, this is the time for which we volunteered to come to planet earth. This is the Age of Aquarius and many people are still carrying the baggage of fear, doubt and records of death from Pisces. These vibrations cannot go forward into a golden age. To understand our initiations in this new time, we must accelerate into Aquarian Age thinking, knowing and being.

We are the heart, head and hands of God in the earth which means we are the doers, the bearers of the Christ Light for bringing in a new day of miracles.

This new time requires us to strive for a balanced threefold fold flame and balance in the four lower bodies. We need an intense third-eye vision and faith because we are being called to believe in and create a level of restoration that surely taxes our acquired belief systems of the last 2,000 years. We know the Father's law; we have heard the prophecies that predict the consequences of being outside the law. And now we go unto the Mother to gain not only consolation but a greater understanding of just what it will take, how we can go about passing the tests, where to place our energies, when to act and when to be silent, and why there is no other place to be and nothing more important to do than fulfill the law of the Father by the expansion of our hearts' love in action.

And the Mother is faithful to give answer to all our questions and concerns while she supports and reinforces what the Father has decreed. The rosary is our petition, our affirmation of our oneness with the law and the lawgivers, our plea for consolation, our raising up of the light upon the spinal altar which is the comfort we have come to offer this world in the name of the Holy Spirit, the Great Comforter. It is violet fire for the consuming and transmutation of all that never should have been.

The Blessed Mother Mary issues the call to action saying, "Beloved ones of the Light of God that never fails, **pray for this nation and this government; for here is the key to a golden age or here is the key to devastation.** Thus, Love is the key, and Wisdom. All action taken in the arena of international relations and domestic policy must satisfy the demand of awareness. Only

Christ-awareness produces right action. All of the arguments, right and left, must come to naught, for the Truth that sets men free comes through awareness of God applied through the Universal Christ to the affairs in this octave.

"**Seek God and live. Follow the path of Jesus** to study and learn. Intensify the Light of the heart. Then offer thyself to thy nation, thy world, thy community."[60]

"**Let your celebration of the rosaries, then, in coming days and weeks and months be for the protection of this nation under God and your respective nations. All know that should America go down, beloved, [the nations will ask:] 'Where shall any other nation appear? Therefore, wherever you come from, from wherever you hail, beloved, remember that America must not be allowed to fail or go down.**

"And fail she will and go down she will if the majority of the people have their way with abortion on demand. This, then, remains the Achilles' heel of America today.

"See, then, that you pray with all of your heart and your might that those who have this in their hearts and those who would make it a universal law and availability for all womankind on the planet are barred from positions of leadership. [For these] should be occupied by those who come bearing some portion of the mantle of their Holy Christ Self, some portion of the mantle of my Son.

"In the hours and weeks ahead, then, I want you to remember that I am at your side, assisting you in resolving all things and doing so as quickly as you are able—[that is,] as quickly as you are able to surrender and enter in to the largess of heart of that burning fire of the flame of Jesus, as quickly as you are able to pass your fingers over the notes (and especially the wrong notes) of your own psychology and play the right notes and then to seal that chord of harmony in your being, to seal it, protect it and not allow it again to be violated anywhere, anytime by any person.

"Hold fast what thou hast received! Keep your eyes open. **Keep your heart in the secret love star of Venus, where many of you have come from.** Preserve the Teaching, first by assimilating it and [then by] radiating it to an entire world."[61]

As I was writing the final pages of this Rosary, the earth experienced the transit of Venus passing by the Sun on June 5, 2012, a very powerful energetic point. The previous transit of Venus took place on June 8, 2004 and the next pair of transits will occur December 10-11, 2117 and in December 2125. By this time, the future of America as a pilot nation bearing the Light of the Christ to all the nations of earth will have outplayed, and that future is in the hands of the lighterbearers of planet earth right now.

The America Rosary to Unite the I AM Race is a devotional ritual designed to be given alone or with others at any time or place of your choosing. It is designed to assist the body of unascended lightbearers in every nation to succeed in making good on the pledge of oneness and unity to physically manifest God-reality throughout the nations of the earth and to bring Earth into the fulfillment of her divine plan as Freedom's Star. A requirement for this victory is that America, as a pilot nation, fulfills her divine plan and provides the blueprint anchored for all nations to gravitate to their rightful "place in the sun." And as we have learned, the key to the victory is to flood America with a sea of violet fire.

This Rosary is an offering that we can all cooperate in bringing to life. An Aquarian Age of restoration and miracles requires cooperation, right alliance and harmony instead of competition and divisiveness. Together, we of many nations can be unified as an alliance for Light. We are the sons and daughters of God moving forward on the quest for our holy communion with God and with God in each other. We do this by residing in the heart of the Mother to produce the Will of the Father. Our pledge of unity to consume and transmute the records of darkness, infamy, betrayal and war by the power of the violet fire within the rosary is a demonstration of our Love for the Power of the Father and the Wisdom of the Mother.

This Rosary has four components or aspects representing the four personality aspects of God (Father, Son, Holy Spirit and Mother) and the four sides of the pyramid being constructed to receive the capstone.

Our steadfast offering of this Rosary is the surrendering of selfishness that allows us as initiates to forge the individual God Mastery that shapes the white cube in our hearts. Our striving for oneness and working in unity creates the mystery of the placement of the capstone—that is, that even though it is made of individual white cubes, it becomes the single capstone that can never be taken apart. And our constancy in invoking the Rosary becomes the reinforcement needed to continue releasing the memories of our Piscean Age lifetime dramas of a path of sorrow, suffering, and sense of aloneness or separateness from God. Instead we are reaffirming our oneness with God, with one another and with the consciousness of the Aquarian Age way of being in this world.

Each aspect begins with the call to Our Father and contains thirteen recitations of the Word (scripture, teachings of the masters and messengers, and affirmations derived from the teachings intended for the Aquarian Age) that initiate the law that the call compels the answer. Each recitation is followed by a Hail Mary that is modified to focus on "America's victorious ascension in the Light." Each of us is reminded to think of America both as the nation of the United States of America, and as the America which represents all of the I AM Race as we offer this version of the Hail Mary. The thirteen recitations represent the twelve tribes, the twelve Apostles plus the Christ in the center. Affirmations follow to seal each of the aspects.

As we recite our affirmations, we understand that the words "I AM" represent the use of the name of God and it means "God in me is." Therefore, when we decree *I AM the Resurrection and the Life of the I AM Race,* we are saying, *God in me is the Resurrection and the Life of the I AM Race.*

Let us lead with the Flame of Victory! Let us pledge to God and to God in one another that we will not be separated by the Gog and Magog forces of darkness abroad in the earth, and that we will unite in invoking the Word so that *they shall not pass!* Let us manifest the Unity of the Divine Intent!

The Ascended Master El Morya, Chief of the Darjeeling Council, has addressed us saying, "To Our Best Outposts, Courage!

"The way made plain has different meanings to individuals. Midst the diversities of human thought, always bear in mind the unity of the divine intent. The Orbs of Truth, supposedly obvious, is reflected in the pool of maya and thereby takes on human distortions—but only in the reflected image.

"Honor, justice, loyalty, and truth have only one meaning, and those whose mouths are set to utter forth this meaning will likewise pursue the divine intent. Such as these can be relied upon in every crisis. Godlike, they do not fail.

"The unhorsing of a rider need not prevent a stalwart remounting of the steed of divine purpose nor the victory over every opposition. This is Armageddon!

"Let me again make clear the words of the Christ: 'Beware when all men speak well of you, for so did their fathers to the false prophets.' As the battle intensifies in man and society wherein striving for a golden age continues, our best outposts, who strike telling blows for the Lord, shall suffer attack.

"Rally, then, as never before and in every way! Our banner goes before you. On it is emblazoned the Will of God.

"In unity of strength shall we implant this banner upon the Summit. You do not know the meaning of unconditional dedication until you give it! To us it is solidarity, victory, and courage to face the dragons that seek to mutilate the image of Christ.

"Forward, Morya."[62]

Part 2

Saint Germain Implores Sanat Kumara

*H*Prayer to Sanat Kumara by our ever devoted friend and God of Freedom, Saint Germain from a dictation titled *Our Service in the next Hundred Years of America's Destiny.* **Saint Germain invoked these Words on December 11, 1977:**

"O Lord Sanat Kumara, I am here with these souls who have declared the freedom and the victory. I am here, Sanat Kumara, and they have responded, and they will not betray America. I know they will not! I implore you, Sanat Kumara, to release now into our hearts the flame of the original signing of the Declaration of Independence as we meditate upon Independence hall and go there to the very cradle of our liberty.

"So we assemble as the early patriots. We assemble together as statesmen ascended, unascended. We come in consciousness. We come to hear the call, 'Sign that document!' We come to ratify the thirteen. We come to declare that this nation ought to be and is indeed a free people, a sovereign nation, one that is conceived in liberty.

"Ancient of Days, O Sanat Kumara, let us be one, then, in this moment, and let our hearts' energies be multiplied by the powers of a cosmos, by their wisdom, and by their love that we might not surrender this blessed earth.

"I kneel before Almighty God this day. I kneel before the altar of freedom and I ask once again for those dispensations of freedom. I beg you, Almighty God, not to say no to me, for I am your son of freedom and I have brought with me to our altar sons and daughters of freedom. And if, O God, all dispensations that I have called forth have been misused by mankind and if, O LORD, you will not hear my plea, then I say, Hear the plea of these embodied souls! Hear their cry, O God! Receive their causal bodies and know that I no longer stand alone on earth, but there are those with me who will not surrender to the tyrant's will, who will surrender only to God.

"And I know, O LORD, by thy name and by thy flame, these too can conquer in Christ's name. These too can go forth as we went forth of old. These too can cast the writing on the wall that is not a spell of darkness but is the writing of the victors bold. O LORD, I implore you by our fervent cry, send forth the instrument! Send forth the lightbearers! Send forth the army! Send forth the light that will crystallize, crystallize the Mind of God and the heart of God and turn this nation into a miracle of joy and light ascending.

"I thank thee, O God. I thank thee for the opportunity to pray this day. I thank thee for the opportunity to stand on earth and to come to this glorious city where the saints have walked, where the pilgrims have known the inspiration of Mother Liberty. I thank thee, O God, for Opportunity, my own twin flame, who has extended that flame throughout a cosmos. And in the moments of discouragement when freedom seemed lost, I thank thee for her aspiration of the feminine consciousness of opportunity whereby I could try and try again to work with mankind for the victory.

"I thank thee for the Mother on high and the Mother below. I thank thee that there have been many ascended masters who have taken their stand with me and who have pledged their love. I thank thee, O God, in thy name, in the name of the Father and the Son and the Holy Spirit and in the name of the Blessed Virgin."[63] AMEN!

AMERICA Rosary to Unite the I AM RACE

[Mantras marked with an asterisk (*) are to be given 3 or 9 times.]

[**Optional:** Meditate on the music *Finlandia* by Sibelius, the keynote of Sanat Kumara, or on the *Ave Maria* by Charles Gounod. You may also choose to sing songs to Saint Germain, Mother Mary and Jesus.]

_____

_____

Invocation:

In the holy name, I AM THAT I AM and the mighty I AM Presence of each one, come forth legions of the Archangels, Elohim, Chohans of the Rays, and Cosmic Beings to clear the way for the Presence of Sanat Kumara, the Holy Kumaras, Saint Germain, Mother Mary and Jesus the Christ, the Fourteen Ascended Masters who govern the destiny of America, the Goddess of Liberty, all those serving the Violet Flame, and Mighty Victory! O God of Freedom, the universal God of all life, come forth! Raise up freedom and let the flame of freedom speak where I AM THAT I AM. Heal the breech in the consciousness of the people. Heal the condition of war. Heal the governments and the economies of each and every nation. Consume all that is anti-Life, including abortion and euthanasia. Heal the sense of separation and remove all doubt and fear.

In the name of the living word, in the name of Saint Germain, let the full fire of freedom appear! Let liberty appear! Let the Violet Flame angels descend and let there be a great stirring in the hearts of the people worldwide! And let Freedom transmute all that is anti-Light! To these ends, I do decree...

Optional Insert Invocation—Compose your personal prayer for you and your family, America, your nation and all the nations of Terra: _____

_____

Sign of the Cross and Consecration

In the name of the Ancient of Days, Sanat Kumara, the I AM THAT I AM, in the name of the Father, the Son and the Holy Spirit, and the Divine Mother, I AM consecrating AMERICA as the Twelve Tribes of the Lost House of Israel, the 144,000, and the I AM Race to the Immaculate Heart of Mary.

In the name, Jesus Christ, I consecrate America, Russia and every nation on earth to the Immaculate Heart of Mary!

In the Immaculate Heart of Mary, I trust.*

ASPECT 1: *I AM THAT I AM and the Twelve Tribes*

I AM LORD'S PRAYER by Jesus Christ:[64]

Our Father who art in heaven,
Hallowed be Thy name, I AM.
I AM Thy kingdom come
I AM Thy will being done
I AM on earth even as I AM in heaven
I AM giving this day daily bread to all
I AM forgiving all life this day even as
I AM also all life forgiving me
I AM leading all men away from temptation
I AM delivering all men from every evil condition
I AM the kingdom
I AM the power and
I AM the glory of God in eternal, immortal manifestation—
All this I AM.

Hail Mary

Hail Mary, full of Grace
The Lord is with Thee.
Blessed art thou among women
And blessed is the fruit of thy womb, Jesus.
Holy Mary, Mother of God
Pray for us sons and daughters of God
Now and at the hour of America's
Victorious ascension in the Light.

"I am of the house of Israel! I am of one of the twelve tribes! I come to return the tribes to the one God! I come to rescue all who have gone out of the way! I come as the instrument of the Cosmic Virgin to support the work of the World Mother and her emissaries in this age."[65]

56

Hail Mary...

I AM One with Lord Maitreya who comes "to restore the Christhood of America," meaning America as the I AM Race embodied in every nation, in every race, in every area of the planet.[66]

Hail Mary...

I AM expanding my horizons as I see "the map of the earth, the solar system, the galaxy and claim it all for the seed of Sanat Kumara. There is no limitation in the heart of Alpha" regarding my own calling except that which I should retain in consciousness.[67]

Hail Mary...

I AM One with the Ascended Hosts who "come first and foremost to restore the lightbearers of America and the world, to that God-estate of" our "individual Sonship."[68]

Hail Mary...

One with the Mighty I AM Presence, I seek the 144,000, "those who have covered the face of the earth with the very special vibration of the understanding of ascended master law that was written in their inward parts long ago when they were with Moses, and long before that when they were with Sanat Kumara."[69]

Hail Mary...

I AM One with Saint Patrick who "has come to help us make contact with the lightbearers of all nations, to alert them to the message, to alert them to the teachings of the ascended masters, to bring them together so that they can form the nucleus for the victory and the salvation of earth. Until we make this contact, identify our brotherhood, identify our community, we do not sense our strength."[70]

Hail Mary...

I AM called to be a son of God, a daughter of God, and to convey the message to the prisoners of the respective nations—"prisoners in the sense that they are bound by certain customs and laws and political and religious ideologies, whereby they have forgotten the one true law of the I AM THAT I AM."[71]

Hail Mary...

I AM one with Igor, the Russian Saint "who kept the vigil with the Blessed Mother of Jesus during the Bolshevik revolution," and in "keeping that tie to the Blessed Mother did prevent untold millions [from perishing] who would have been engaged in bloodshed and would have [indeed] perished."[72]

Hail Mary...

"I AM One with Pallas Athena. I AM Greek. I AM Roman. I AM freeborn. I AM a member of every nation. I AM an American. From this day and forevermore, I espouse the cause of truth."[73]

Hail Mary...

"In the living flame of truth, I am grateful for love of truth, of liberty, for courage and self-sacrifice. I AM grateful, and I bow before the flame of truth within myself and within all whom I meet."[74]

Hail Mary...

"And I will use that flame to light my nation and to light a world!"[75]

Hail Mary...

"Thus, this is the new nation of the people of Israel conceived in liberty. This is liberty: to know the truth that the truth might make you free."[76]

Hail Mary...

"This is the land of a free people—a people who are free, not unto themselves, but a people who are the guardians of freedom to the earth."[77]

Hail Mary...

I AM the new nation of the people of Israel conceived in liberty!*

Praise the Lord I AM THAT I AM, Sanat Kumara!*

A - U - M

ASPECT 2: *Jesus the Christ and the Individualized Christ of the Sons and Daughters of God*

The I AM Lord's Prayer...

Hail Mary...

In the name, Jesus Christ, I consecrate America, Russia and every nation on earth to the Immaculate Heart of Mary!

In the Immaculate Heart of Mary, I trust!*

"I and the Father are One."[78] As I affirm this, I understand that the Father has already said, I and My Son are one. And this longing of God for oneness is like the longing of the pyramid for its capstone.

Hail Mary...

As I declare that I and my Father are One, I lose myself in service, watch my thoughts, trace my feelings and eradicate selfishness by the violet flame.[79]

Hail Mary...

As I truly become one with the Father, I know that I AM One with all of His sons and daughters in manifestation, and I begin to experience that Oneness as the forging of the white cube in my heart.[80]

Hail Mary...

I AM One with my Lord and Savior, Jesus Christ who decreed, "I AM the Way, the Truth and the Life."[81]

Hail Mary...

"Verily, verily, I say unto you, He that believeth on me, the works that I do shall he do also; and greater works than these shall he do; because I go unto my Father."[82]

Hail Mary...

I AM One with the disciples at Pentecost, and I receive and claim the commission to be divinely empowered with extraordinary faith, knowledge, and ability, to develop steadfastness in faithfulness, tremendous transformation in my person, a total submission to the Holy Spirit even in the midst of great tribulations, and a willingness to be used continuously and unconditionally by God.

Hail Mary…

I AM One with a worldwide body, both ascended and unascended, that is called the Great White Brotherhood. And as a body of lightbearers, we strive together in Oneness and Unity to provide the building blocks for the capstone and the All Seeing Eye of God.

Hail Mary…

I AM One with those who keep the Flame of Freedom and Liberty on Earth, along with all Ascended Masters, Archangels, Cosmic Beings, Buddhas, Bodhisattvas, Elohim, elementals and the tiniest angel, my own body elemental.

Hail Mary…

I claim the mantra of my Lord Jesus Christ, *for judgment I AM come.* For resolution I AM come. I AM come for the resolution of the not-self and the anti-Christ with the Holy Christ Self and the Mighty I AM Presence.

Hail Mary…

With men in their lesser selves, it is impossible, but not with God. "For with God, all things are possible."[83]

Hail Mary…

"All who desire that Christ, all who have the capacity to see that Christ will love you and will come unto you because you raise it up. And then…because you raise it up, all who have enmity with Christ, all who hate that Christ will revile you: they will persecute you, they will do it again and again."[84]

Hail Mary…

I AM surrendering my procrastination of my Christhood, which is here and now a cosmic reality.

Hail Mary...

In this battle, men, women and children of faith in God are standing together. Victory is everywhere in the consciousness of God!

Hail Mary...

I and the Father are One!*

I must work the works of Him that sent me!*

I come in Love, with the legions of the Archangels to challenge those who organize on a world scale and an interstellar scale to fight against God, against religion, against peace, against true Brotherhood and who would sow chaos, confusion, suspicion and hatred to set man against man. Be gone, forces of anti-Love!*

A – U – M

ASPECT 3: *AMERICA as the I AM Race*

The I AM Lord's Prayer...

Hail Mary...

In the name, Jesus Christ, I consecrate America, Russia and every nation on earth to the Immaculate Heart of Mary!

In the Immaculate Heart of Mary, I trust!*

"The children of Israel are of every race and nation and religion. They are not confined to any one race. This is the I AM race. The I AM race is one with every Keeper of the Flame; there is no distinction."[85]

Hail Mary...

"The children of Israel are the sons and daughters of God who have appeared again and again throughout the ages."[86]

Hail Mary...

Beloved Pallas Athena has decreed: "We look upon your profiles. We look into your auras. We see you as you came out of Egypt, out of the land of bondage, as you compromised not the flame of freedom, as you were willing to surrender all possessions, all comfortability, all ways of life that was known to move toward the unknown. That record is within you."[87]

Hail Mary...

I challenge and I dispel by the power of the Spoken Word the forgetfulness that God is in me, forgetfulness of the power of the Word, forgetfulness that I AM One with the prophets and the messengers who have embraced me with their hearts, souls and minds and therefore I cannot be divided from God.[88]

Hail Mary...

I reject the plot of the fallen consciousness that would have me believe the lie of separateness, aloneness and apartness.

Hail Mary...

I AM One with AMERICA through the heart chakra! I AM One with AMERICA through the threefold flame! I AM One with AMERICA through the Secret Chamber of the Heart!

Hail Mary...

I AM an American and I proclaim Freedom and Liberty in every nation.

Hail Mary...

"This earth must have knowledge! Woman must have self-knowledge; man must have self-knowledge and the child must know the Inner Christ as the Holy Christ Self and the Inner Buddha as the I AM THAT I AM."[89]

Hail Mary...

I AM the witness of the living body of God on the earth now. I will not postpone my service until I am perfected for then I will no longer be in this earth and I will not be as useful in this plane.

Hail Mary...

In the face of the fallen ones who come to confront and tell me, *You cannot deliver this world in this age*, I do give answer: "I never said that it was I who would deliver the world in this age. For it is God in me who will do that work and I AM worthy."[90]

Hail Mary...

I AM responding to the summons to be a witness unto Jesus Christ in this age, "for the securing of the Great City Foursquare in North America—the promised land to which the 144,000 are called" and galvanized "to go forth for the awakening of America and every nation."[91]

64

Hail Mary...

I AM surrendering into the violet flame my human selfishness, which is the great barrier to the bringing in of the Golden Age in America and on Terra.

Hail Mary...

I and my nation are centered in selflessness "which gives forth the light, the protection, the perfection of the defense of freedom in every nation upon earth where freedom is threatened by the dragon of World Communism."[92]

Hail Mary...

It is God in me that will do that work and I AM worthy!*

I AM the Resurrection and the Life of the I AM Race!*

Jesus Christ, the same Yesterday and Today and Forever!*

A - U - M

ASPECT 4: *The Power of the Divine Mother Wedded to the Holy Spirit!*

The I AM Lord's Prayer...

Hail Mary...

In the name, Jesus Christ, I consecrate America, Russia and every nation on earth to the Immaculate Heart of Mary!

In the Immaculate Heart of Mary, I trust!*

I surrender my vulnerability in selfishness as I aspire to selflessness. I accept my responsibility to be. I accept the components of my reality. I accept the flame of God within me.

Hail Mary...

I bow before the Lord God Almighty and I affirm that I am his beloved son, his beloved daughter. I accept my immortal destiny. I accept my reason for being.

Hail Mary...

I see my divine plan "in light of the burden of" my family and my nation as they are my karma. And I "do not fiddle while Rome burns" or "look for other diversions or pursuits" while "our people suffer and our nation must be delivered."[93]

Hail Mary...

In the name of Beloved Mother Mary, "I come in the way of the Aquarian Age. I come to America. I come to Terra." And "I come releasing the electronic presence of my momentum of attainment in the threefold flame."[94]

Hail Mary...

As I draw forth the energies of the Divine Mother, I hold in my hand "the key to the victory of a civilization," leading the energies of life and disciplining those energies.[95]

Hail Mary...

I AM poised to stand with the Divine Mother to stand, face and conquer "the dragon of the carnal mind that occupies" my own "feeling world" and my own "mental world."[96]

Hail Mary...

In the name of Sanat Kumara, I have "the authority of the rod of Aaron" to "exorcise those beasts of consciousness," and when I "have triumphed over the beasts within," I go forth with other heroes and "heroines of the cause of the Brotherhood."[97]

Hail Mary...

I AM raising up the Mother ray "who prepares the soul, initiates the light and the cycles, holds the blueprint, knows in her heart that her son and her daughter will overcome, will fulfill the law," and "will return to the heart of the One."[98]

Hail Mary...

God has decided to save the earth! "I am the child of Liberty. I live in Liberty. I send forth liberty to all. I am but a child and so these simple words that God has decided to save the earth are enough for me."[99]

Hail Mary...

"I live in the comfort of the Lord God of Hosts. I am nestled in his cosmos. I am secure in starlight, in sunshine, in the wind and in the rain. I am secure because God made me and because I know he is in me."[100]

Hail Mary...

One with Mighty Elohim Astrea, I go forth determined "that this earth shall ascend as Freedom's Star," and I "go forth into the community of the world at large to deliver the mandate of freedom for souls to live and breathe on Terra."[101]

Hail Mary...

I AM beholding the alchemy of "Saint Germain and Jesus in the turning around of events," and I AM reading "the record written in living letters of gold of this one truth" – I AM "the Christ incarnate now."[102]

Hail Mary...

I AM standing with our blessed Mother Mary. And I recite the Rosary daily so that the Hail Mary and the calls that we make for the many nations of the earth might bear fruit and give strength to every heart.

Hail Mary...

Let the fiat of the Lord Saint Germain be with me!*

Come Divine Mother. Come Holy Child. Come Holy Spirit so gentle, so mild.*

In the name I AM THAT I AM, I call for the Christic pattern of the founding of this Nation under God to be manifest in me! And with Mother Omega, I call for the lightbearers' full and final declaration of independence from the fallen ones!*

Lightbearers of the world unite, in the name of Saint Germain!*

I AM the Resurrection and the Life of the I AM Race!*

Praise the Lord I AM THAT I AM, Sanat Kumara!*

Sign of the Cross and Sealing:

In the name of the Father, the Son, the Holy Spirit and the Mother, it is done, it is finished, it is sealed! For the mouth of the Lord hath spoken it! Amen.

*And in full faith, I consciously accept this manifest, manifest, manifest (*3x), right here and now with full power eternally sustained, all powerfully active, ever expanding and world enfolding until all are wholly ascended in the light and free. Beloved I AM, Beloved I AM, Beloved I AM.[103]

A - U - M

End Notes

ll end note references from copyrighted materials from Church Universal and Triumphant (C.U.T.), The Summit Lighthouse, Summit University Press and the Radiant Word are reprinted with permission. Gratitude is extended for these resources and courtesy. Throughout these notes PoW stands for Pearls of Wisdom, weekly publications of the ascended master dictations and the messengers' lectures. Ordering or contact information: PO Box 5000, Gardiner, MT 59030; 406-848-9500; Website: www.tsl.org; Email: tslinfo@tsl.org

Readers are encouraged to pursue greater illumination by studying these resources in depth.

---

[1] Lanello, June 2, 1985, "Moving Forward," in *PoW*, Vol. 28 No. 27, July 7, 1985, Copyright © C.U.T.

[2] Archangel Uriel and Aurora, July 15, 1990, Freedom 1990 - A New Heaven and a New Earth – VIII, "The Christic Pattern of the Founding of the Nation; You Must Make the Call and the Call Will Be Answered! Omega Descends with the Judgment of Those Who Oppose the Divine Manchild and the Woman; The Lightbearers' Full and Final Declaration of Independence from the Fallen Ones," in *PoW*, Vol. 33 No. 27, Copyright © C.U.T.

[3] http://www.ewtn.com/devotionals/prayers/rosary/how_to.htm

[4] Email: tslinfo@tsl.org

[5] Ibid.

[6] Caritas of Birmingham; 205-672-2000, Ext. 315

[7] This is not a reference to race as ethnicity but refers to the Saints robed in White.

[8] E.C. Prophet, September 27, 1998, "Update on Fàtima and Medjugorje, Celebrations of the Fortieth Anniversary of the Founding of the Summit Lighthouse - 1," in *PoW* Vol. 41 No. 39, Copyright © C.U.T.

[9] E.C. Prophet, (Speaker). *A Child's Rosary to Mother Mary*, various recorded albums, Copyright © The Summit Lighthouse for C.U.T.

[10] A Friend of Medjugorje, September 11, 2003; Two Americas, pp. 13-14. Copyright © SJP International 2004, 2006, 2007, 2009, SJP.

[11] Lord Maitreya with Arcturus and Victoria, May 11, 1986, Teachings from the Mystery School X - "I Draw the Line!" in *PoW*, Vol. 29 No. 19, Copyright © C.U.T.

[12] Saint Germain, July 4, 1975, *The Great White Brotherhood in the Culture, History and Religion of America*, July 4, 1975, "A Confirmation of Freedom," p. 161, Copyright © 1975, 1976, 1977, 1983, Summit University Press.

[13] Saint Germain, April 7, 2012, "The Lord's Prophecy unto the Philippines by Saint Germain," in *PoW*, Vol. 28 No. 14, Copyright © C.U.T.

[14] Omri-Tas, June 29, 1988, Saint Germain Stumps Portugal 2 - A Reservoir of Violet Flame over Europe - "A New Vision and a New Quickening Must Come," in *PoW*, Vol. 31 No. 33, Copyright © C.U.T.

[15] Lanello, December 24, 1988, PoW, Vol. 31 No. 86, The Spirit of the Great White Brotherhood, "A Candle in the Night," in *PoW*, Vol. 31 No. 86, Copyright © C.U.T.

[16] Portia, July 17, 1988, Saint Germain Stumps America 21, "The Mother of Aquarius Steps Down from Cosmic Levels - As You Receive Me, Earth Shall Become Freedom's Star," in *PoW*, Vol. 31 No. 86, Copyright © C.U.T.

[17] Elohim Heros and Amora, March 19, 1978, Spoken by Elohim Out of the Spirit of the LORD unto the Two Witnesses, *Behold, Our God Is a Consuming Fire of Love!*, in *PoW*, Vol. 21 No. 12, Copyright © C.U.T.

[18] Sanat Kumara, June 6, 1999, Ghana Class 1976, "Rekindling the Threefold Flame on the Continent of Afra," in *PoW*, Vol. 42 No. 23, Copyright © C.U.T.

[19] Peter Marshall and David Manuel, *The Light and the Glory 1492-1793*, p. 15, published by Revell (www.revellbooks.com). Copyright © 1977, 2009 by Peter J. Marshall, Jr. and David B. Manuel Jr.

[20] Great Divine Director, March 29, 1970, Class of the Resurrection Flame, Santa Barbara, CA.

[21] Luke 12:48.

[22] Saint Germain, May 22, 1979, "To Our Gracious Readers, Dedicated to Love's Service the World Around," in *PoW*, Vol. 2 No. 20, Copyright 1999 © C.U.T.

[23] Saint Germain, August 14, 1977, Saint Germain on Freedom II – "The Grand Adventure, Part 2," in *PoW*, Vol. 20 No. 33, Copyright © C.U.T.

[24] E. C. Prophet, *The Great White Brotherhood in the Culture, History and Religion of America*, Introduction, pp.v-vii. Copyright © Summit University Press 1975, 1976, 1977, 1983.

[25] Peter Marshall and David Manuel, *The Light and the Glory 1492-1793*, pp. 14-15, published by Revell (www.revellbooks.com). Copyright © 1977, 2009 by Peter J. Marshall, Jr. and David B. Manuel Jr.

[26] Ibid.

[27] Ibid.

[28] Andy Andrews, *How Do You Kill 11 MILLION PEOPLE? Why the Truth Matters More Than You Think*, p. 52, Copyright © 2011 Andy Andrews, ISBN: 978-1-4041-8356-8 (IE), SpecialMarkets@ThomasNelson.com

[29] Ibid. Summary on copyright page

[30] Saint Germain, December 11, 1983, Discover the New Age with Saint Germain – I – "The Resolution of the Darjeeling Council, The History of the I AM Race," in *PoW*, Vol. 26 No. 50, Copyright © C.U.T.

[31] Ibid.

[32] Ibid.

[33] Mother Mary, July 29, 1973, "Communion Feast at the Temple of the Resurrection with Mary, Jesus, and Lanello, Part II," in *PoW*, Vol. 16 No. 30, 1973. Copyright © C.U.T.

72

34 Buddha of the Ruby Ray, December 6, 1992, Shafts of Ruby Ray for Transmutation and for the Rising of the Divine Mother in the South – You Are a Mighty People from Atlantis Come Again – "To Know, to Dare, to Do and to Be Silent" Is Your Motto." in PoW, Vol. 35 No. 63, Copyright © C.U.T.

35 El Morya, January 31, 1993, One Voice – The Cause that is America, in PoW, Vol. 36 No. 5, Copyright © C.U. T.

36 Ibid.

37 E.C. Prophet, February 11, 1990, Prophecy for the 1990's III, "The Four Horsemen: A 2,000-Year Ride," in PoW, Vol. 33 No. 6, Copyright © C.U.T.

38 El Morya, September 23, 1984, A Study in Christhood by the Great Initiator – XLII, "Message to America on the Mission of Jesus Christ," in PoW, Vol. 27 No. 47, Copyright © C.U.T.

39 Saint Germain, February 17, 1980, The Economic Survival of the Nations, in PoW, Vol. 23 No. 7, Copyright © C.U.T.

40 Rev. Peter J. Marshall, Editor, The Wartime Sermons of Dr. Peter Marshall, Clarion Call Marketing, Inc. PO Box 610010, Dallas, TX 526. Copyright © 2005 Rev. Peter J. Marshall, First Edition.

41 Ibid.

42 Ibid.

43 El Morya, September 23, 1984, A Study in Christhood by the Great Initiator – XLII, "Message to America on the Mission of Jesus Christ," in PoW, Vol. 27 No. 47, Copyright © C.U.T.

44 America's God and Country, Encyclopedia of Quotations; William J. Federer; Amerisearch, Inc.; Copyright © 2000 by William J. Federer.

45 Saint Germain, July 5, 1981, "The Mosaic of Life," in PoW, Vol. 24 No. 27, Copyright 1981 © C.U.T.

46 Archangel Uriel, December 2, 1987, In Defense of the People of God, "The Good Karma of the I AM Race—Defend Your Right to Be," Copyright © C.U.T.

[47] Gautama Buddha, June 12, 1977, "Thoughtform for the Year 1977: A Golden Eagle from the God Star Sirius," in *PoW*, Vol. 20 No. 24, Copyright © C.U.T.

[48] Lord Maitreya, October 11, 1992, "To Restore the Christhood of America! Return to the One God – The Question Is Not Can You but Will You Turn the World Around?" in *PoW*, Vol. 35 No. 24, Copyright © C.U.T.

[49] Archangel Michael, July 11, 1982, "Because You Need Me," in *PoW*, Vol. 25 No. 28, Copyright © C.U.T.

[50] Archangel Zadkiel, March 3, 1996, The Messenger Stumps South America – 3 – Zadkiel Appoints Six Violet-Flame Angels to Each One in Attendance, *"Saint Germain Sends His messenger and the Seven Archangel to South America to Inaugurate the Aquarian Age on Earth,* Part 2, in *PoW*, Vol. 39 No. 10, Copyright © C.U.T.

[51] E.C. Prophet, June 18, 1989, Freedom 1988, Fourth of July Address, Part 1, "The Signing of the Declaration of Independence and George Washington's Vision," in *PoW*, Vol. 32 No. 25, Copyright © C.U.T.

[52] Saint Germain, December 16, 1986, "A Prophecy of Karma of the United States of America, Thanksgiving Day Address 1986" in *PoW*, Vol. 29 No. 75, Copyright © C.U.T.

[53] Cyclopea and Sanat Kumara, March 23, 1980, The Mystery of the Capstone, given at Summit University, Copyright © The Radiant Word

[54] Ibid.

[55] Micah, Angel of Unity, April 21, 2002, "Unity is Everything," in *PoW*, Vol. 45 No. 16, Copyright © C.U.T.

[56] Ibid.

[57] Micah, Angel of Unity, October 5, 1962, from Vol. V No. 40, Copyright © Summit Publications.

[58] Saint Germain, December 30, 1972, "The New Order of the Ages," in *PoW*, Vol. 16 No. 52, Copyright © C.U.T.

[59] Mighty Victory, February 2/27/2000, "The Victory Way of Life," in *PoW*, Vol. 43 No. 9, Copyright © C.U.T.

74

[60] Mother Mary, December 29, 1974, A Trilogy of the Mother—The Initiation of the Fusion of Solar Energies - III, in *PoW*, Vol. 17 No. 52, Copyright © C.U.T.

[61] Mother Mary, August 8, 1992, Mother Mary's Ascension Day Address 1992. "Be Careful! Hold Fast to Me. A Perpetual Rosary to the Immaculate Heart of Mary. Balance All Things. Sons and Daughters, Hear Me Well!" in *PoW*, Vol. 35 No. 34, Copyright © C.U.T.

[62] El Morya, August 1, 1965, The Unity of Divine Intent, "To Our Best Outposts, Courage!" in *PoW*, Vol. 8 No. 31, Copyright © Summit publications at C.U.T.

[63] Saint Germain, December 11, 1977, Saint Germain on Freedom XI: *Our Service in the next Hundred Years of America's Destiny*, Part 1, *PoW*, Vol. 20 No. 50, Copyright © C.U.T.

[64] Released by Elizabeth Clare Prophet, I AM Lord's Prayer by Jesus Christ, "Watch with Me" Jesus' Vigil of the Hours, p. 41, Copyright © C.U.T.

[65] Lord Maitreya, October 11, 1992, FREEDOM 1992 "Joy in the Heart" XVII, "To Restore the Christhood of America! Return to the One God. The Question Is Not Can You but Will You Turn the World Around?" in *PoW*, Vol. 35, No. 42, Copyright © C.U.T.

[66] Ibid.

[67] Lanello, November 21, 1987, "The Father's Love," in *PoW*, Vol. 30 No. 52, Copyright © C.U.T.

[68] Lord Maitreya, October 11, 1992, FREEDOM 1992 "Joy in the Heart" XVII, "To Restore the Christhood of America! Return to the One God. The Question Is Not Can You but Will You Turn the World Around?" in *PoW*, Vol. 35, No. 42, Copyright © C.U.T.

[69] Pallas Athena, April 29, 2001, Higher Consciousness, "America: Ye Shall Know the Truth and the Truth Shall Make You Free," in *PoW*, Vol. 44 No 17, Copyright © C.U.T.

[70] Mark L. Prophet and Elizabeth Clare Prophet, The Path of Brotherhood, pp. 144-145, Copyright 2003 by Summit University Press.

[71] Mark L. Prophet and Elizabeth Clare Prophet, The Path of Brotherhood, p. 145, Copyright 2003 by Summit university Press.

75

72 Lord Maitreya, October 11, 1992, FREEDOM 1992 "Joy in the Heart" XVII, "To Restore the Christhood of America! Return to the One God. The Question Is Not Can You but Will You Turn the World Around?" in *PoW*, Vol. 35, No. 42, Copyright © C.U.T.

73 Pallas Athena, April 29, 2001, Higher Consciousness, "America: Ye Shall Know the Truth and the Truth Shall Make You Free," in *PoW*, Vol. 44 No 17, Copyright © C.U.T.

74 Ibid.

75 Ibid.

76 Ibid.

77 Ibid.

78 John 10:30.

79 Cyclopea, March 30, 1980, "The Components of the Capstone - To the Blessed Who Would See Him Face to Face," in *PoW*, Vol. 23 No. 13, Copyright © C.U.T.

80 Ibid.

81 John 14:6.

82 John 14:12.

83 Mark 10:27.

84 Lord Maitreya, October 11, 1992, FREEDOM 1992 "Joy in the Heart" XVII, "To Restore the Christhood of America! Return to the One God. The Question Is Not Can You but Will You Turn the World Around?" in *PoW*, Vol. 35, No. 42, Copyright © C.U.T.

85 Pallas Athena, April 29, 2001, Higher Consciousness, "America: Ye Shall Know the Truth and the Truth Shall Make You Free," in *PoW*, Vol. 44 No 17, Copyright © C.U.T.

86 Ibid.

87 Ibid.

88 Lord Maitreya, October 11, 1992, FREEDOM 1992 "Joy in the Heart" XVII, "To Restore the Christhood of America! Return to the One God. The Question Is Not Can You but Will You Turn the World Around?" in *PoW*, Vol. 35, No. 42, Copyright © C.U.T.

[89] Sarasvati, September 1992, "We Do Work! The Only Cure for Earth Is Illumination. We Shall Press Through for a Worldwide Awakening," in *PoW*, Vol. 35 No. 39, 9/92. Copyright © C.U.T.

[90] Sanat Kumara, June 6, 1999, Ghana Class 1976, "Rekindling the Threefold Flame on the Continent of Afra," in *PoW*, Vol. 42 No. 23, Copyright © C.U.T.

[91] Saint Germain, May 1, 1978, A Letter by Saint Germain, Rakoczy Mansion, Transylvania, "I Summon You to Forge a Living Chalice," *PoW disk*, pp 286-290, Copyright © C.U.T.

[92] Saint Germain, November 27, 1977, SAINT GERMAIN ON FREEDOM - X, "The Meaning of Self-Sacrifice, Part 1," in *PoW*, Vol. 20 No. 48, Copyright © C.U.T.

[93] Saint Germain, April 7, 2012, "The Lord's Prophecy unto the Philippines by Saint Germain," in *PoW*, Vol. 28 No. 14, Copyright © C.U.T.

[94] Mother Mary, October 11, 1975, "The Mother Ray as the Instrument of the Soul's Transition into the New Day," in *PoW*, Vol. 23 No. 27, Copyright © The Radiant Word.

[95] Ibid.

[96] Ibid.

[97] Ibid.

[98] Ibid.

[99] Goddess of Liberty, July 4, 1976, "God Has Decided to Save the Earth," in *PoW*, Vol. 30 No. 8, Copyright © Summit Publications

[100] Ibid.

[101] Astrea, May 1, 1977, ENERGY IS GOD III, "Encircling the Body of God with the Circle of Fire," in *PoW*, Vol 20 No. 18, Copyright © C.U.T.

[102] Sanat Kumara, May 16, 1999, Freedom 1978, *Sing a New Song*, 1, "The Summoning of the Servants of God, in *PoW*, Vol. 42 No. 20, Copyright © C.U.T.

[103] Multiple C.U.T. and TSL publications.